CENNAU'S BELL

Poems 1980-2001

Graham Hartill

For Tilly !
welcome to our
garden !
Graham
Summer '16
x !

The Collective Press

Cataloguing In Publication
Data for this book is available from the British
Library

ISBN 1 899449 01 9

Published with the financial support of the
Arts Council of Wales.
&
The Collective

Main Typeface; Gill Sans MT
Type setting by Anvil
Cover design © John Jones
Original drawings by Graham Hartill

Printed and bound in Great Britain by
MWL Digital Solutions, Pontypool.

Cennau's Bell

Introduction

The poems in this book are taken from several collections produced over twenty years; they probably show some kind of movement, more in loops perhaps than any straightforward progress. Though I have used a lot of historical material, it has never been my intention to write historical poems as such, but rather to write from a multiplicity of selves; thus various kinds of voice can be heard in this book, some of which may be mine, and all of them speaking today.

The only way poets can judge their work, it seems to me, is on the basis of whether or not it still intrigues them. This is the basis on which this collection was gathered.

The poems The Vessel Speaks, The Art Of War and After Gododdin were written while working under a fellowship from the Scottish Arts Council; the Lives of the Saints, Tilt and Silver John sequences under bursaries from the Arts Council of Wales. For these opportunities I owe my thanks.

Glan Yr Afon
Winter 2004

Contents

Contents

Contents

Love and other poems:

❧The Voice of Maria Sabina

You have read about me –

the perpetual utterance of my night vigil –

not my words –

you've travelled the length of Mexico
on squawking pissy trains,
the lofty valleys walled by Spain's
estates, the pyramids, the pulpy fangs
of *mezcal*, rows of it, the cauldrons
of the coast where sea-birds
pick the beach of fish

the white hotels
the soldiers standing round their trucks
in every scalding *zocalo*

& I have travelled
       even though I do not own a dollar

I have flown
      above the country

          I am she who waits
              who tries

              who wins

         & I am she
             who thinks
           & who creates

         & I am she
             who heals

                of Sun & Moon

interpreter

& I can read

my life, &
yours

& yours to come

& mine? is nothing, nothing. Know

        my father knew
        & his
        & his
        & I
        & sister Ana Maria

flew one day
while pasturing the animals
our bellies light & taut as balls
with hunger, fingers ripping
at the mushrooms in the ground
& *Teo Nanacatl* flew into our mouths
& souls

        0 the woman lord of clowns am I
                the mushroom says
           ... yes Jesus says
        the woman of the clock am I, he says
        woman Jesus Christ am I, he says
        the thing is true the mushroom says
        cheer up! don't be concerned!
        look at the world
        the world is pretty
        You, my patron mother, mother
                Concepcion
        woman of the whirlpool in the lake am I
        Oh Jesus patron mother, look
        look how it is, dangerous world, dark
                    world
        I'm going to free this, says
        I'm going to dry it out in the sunlight,

says
the government controls us, says
the judge controls us, says
Woman of the Star of God am I
& woman of affairs am I, a lawyer
woman, woman of paper-work
music woman, woman of the hunting dog
I'm going where you spat, Christ
whirling woman of the whirlwind
woman of a sacred & enchanted place

*

When I was 8
I cured my uncle,
then there were others,
many. One, Maria,
had a swollen face
& hands & belly
like she'd burst –
I took her with me on the journey
there where everything
is known.
                    She lived
for 15 years more.

& then I married.
There was no more curing.
Serapio Martinez
gave me children, 1 - 2 - 3,
& then he died. I had to work
the coffee, sew *huipiles*, trade
in blankets, ponchos, pots & pans...

Then 13 years later came Marcio –
curandero, herbalist & drunk.
He gave me 9, & beat them all
& when I turned again to curing,
where he'd failed, he beat me
black & blue, he nearly killed me.

He was murdered in an alley —
one of his women's husband split
his head with a stick...

> *the woman who thunders*
> *I'm the woman who sounds*
> *Spider Woman, Hummingbird Woman*
> *am I, tender woman*
> *woman of big roots am I*
> *woman rooted below the water am I*
> *woman who sprouts, woman like a begonia*
> *I*
> > *am going to the sky*
> > > *for there my paper*
> > > > *there my book remains...*

*

I saw the Book
when curing my sister Ana.

Everything is in the Book.

I saw my son Aurelio's death
already done, the dagger...

deaths... & buried cities...
other murders...

God I saw & God is a gigantic clock
        which holds the universe...

> I'm the woman who stops the world
> the legendary curing woman
>
> she who waits at every railway station
> with the others, shouting, selling
> up & down the platform –
> > "water! enchiladas! parakeets!"

Interpret me.

My words are not my own
or mine alone.

I suffer,
                heal me –
buy my blankets!

Help me fill my children's mouths.

Perhaps when you get back to USA
you send my children books in English, yes?
One day one might get to USA.

I cannot read. I'm old.

But I have travelled – see!

my eyes are like an eagle's,
brighter than the Southern Cross!

                              *

Note: Some of the content of this poem is taken from Maria Sabina, a Mazatec shaman's, 'veleda' or night-vigil of July 12 1958; it is folded into my own observations, and a conversation with a peasant woman, in the Mexican province of Oaxaca. The full text of incantation, running to 85 pages, can be found in R. Gordon Wasson's book Maria Sabina And Her Mazatec Veleda published by Harcourt, Brace, Jovanovitch in 1974.

Maria Sabina died in poverty in 1985 at the age of 97.

The Names of God

Brown Bear

Grizzly Bear

Mongolian Beaver

Chinese Alligator

Nile Crocodile

Giant Catfish

Asiatic Lion

Giant Armadillo

North African Kit Fox

Central and West African Gorilla

Jamaican Boa

American Blue Pike

Mexican Bobcat

San Franciscan Garter Snake

Kangaroo

White Oriental Stork!

and these being just a small

proportion of the endangered

names of God

*

Snow falls. The train from Merthyr

slides along the river, the forestry

luminous brown

Taf river
is a green eel shining
eats names, carries these names
in its gut
towns, people in the towns
faces, people and hill-faces
holographed in the coal-face
gold mountains
brilliant spring sunface

black river, eel river
forever eating
and carrying in its belly, shining
pebbles and plastic bags
                            white
houses terraced slopes to the East
          purple and yellow
and each house
          is a name of god
and each name
          is a crowd

                    *

                    Jesus the eel
                    Jesus the 2 crows
                    Jesus police, Jesus cloud
                    Jesus with his arms full of trees

                    Jesus the cockerel, Jesus the wheel
                    Jesus smoking Jesus swearing Jesus drunk
                    Jesus the high wire, Jesus the coalman

butcher, baker, undertaker
Jesus the busker, Jesus the whisky priest
Jesus the semiconductor
the camera, Jesus the high-heeled shoe

Jesus the factory smoke Jesus
       the fabric of smoke

Jesus the made-up eyes Jesus
       the sunlight

Jesus the blue railway

Jesus the rich milk

Jesus the coarse fur

Jesus the snowy mountain

Jesus the rat

Jesus the hole in the mountain

Jesus the night-blue feather

Jesus purple and yellow

*

Fever Wind

This wind blow hot
        mother, father
this wind blow cold

        so cold it will freeze you

freeze your nerves
        so you'll never grow old
freeze your heart
        so you'll never feel cold

        fever wind singing: sunshine and moonshine
                dry out your bones

this wind blow cold
        brother, sister
wind blow hot

        so hot it will burn you

burn your nostrils
        so you can't smell burning
burn your heart
        so you can't feel a thing

        this fever-wind singing brother, sister
                fever-wind singing sunshine and moonshine
        dry off your hands

                                        *

fever-wind
   is a house on fire
fever-wind
   is a ten-ton truck
fever-wind
   a compulsive liar
fever-wind
   is your good luck

fever-wind
   is a god in the tree-tops
fever-wind
   is a prisoner on the run
fever-wind
   is a word in your ear
fever-wind
   some guy with a gun

fever-wind talks
   and you can't quite catch it
fever-wind laughs
   and you don't know why
fever-wind turns up
   when you least expect it
fever-wind opposite
   catching your eye

*

people will pay good money for a taste of the
                                         wind
it brings pictures loaded with savage flowers
a cargo of animals
and talking birds

    when the fever-wind blows
people collect together
        and try to catch it from each other's mouths

we will pay good money
    for a dose of it
for a blast of
    the fever-wind

    the men wear their brightest dresses
        they look like flowers
the women talk like animals
    the wind blows in and out of their mouths

    our tongues become wild
                blue
                    birds

    when it blows
        trees
                grow in our teeth
            songs
                    yellow and red
                through the windows
                    of broken houses

*

Ghost Dance

the Earth is yellow
the Earth is blue
listen to this rhyme
grandfather
in your scorching nail factory, 1924
listen to my song
grandmother
stringing up rabbit-meat in your grocery shop
doing your accounts

the Earth is brown and wet
there is rain pouring on gaslit streets
take account of this song grandmother
it is pouring with rain

the Earth is white
the Earth is red
the bird may be dead
but the feather is still flying
the whirlwind blew
and your faces became water
the sun still shines on that running water
I can hear you
walking between the stars
I can hear you
patrolling up and down through time
this is
            the Ghost Dance

                            *

– wild stars,
the faces before me.
My father's, strong,
exhausted,
30 years putting doors on cars,
two weeks day-shift,

two weeks night shift,
asks me if I've got a bob or two
and I say yes and he says
you're alright then?
Bear-man, looking after stomachs.

And my mother's, 72
still going strong,
looking after brothers, sisters
through the 30's and the War
with grandad out of work,
her angular, dark and respectable
face in a photo in the dining room,
and later, straight after marriage,
her wartime face.

*

the field is yellow
the field is red
listen to the snow
grandchildren
and to the heat
the field is brown and wet
there is wind in the streets

the sky is green
grandchildren
the sky is white
I wonder where you live?
the ground reclaims its own life

*

this is
        the Ghost Dance
the breadword
the colourword

city of wind
the city of travellers

the city of day
the city of grass

      *

The Vessel Speaks

It's snowing, and below the streets the delta carries forward, discharging its cargo of seeds to the black mud. A river of metallic lights courses up the wet black hill of the city. Faces at tables are reflected in the windows and in the glass cases of the exhibition within which the vessels are settled, squat and rounded: ochre zig-zags, dots and diamonds, black, brick-red, white and grey geometrics - Chavin, Moche and Nazca ceramics, dating 3000 to 250 B.C.

The lost governments of the Earth could be listening in eternity to the list of buried rivers, which is as long as your arm. In this northern city it is Winter. The slides flick past - Monte Alban, Teotihuacán, the great temples of the Sun and Moon. In 1978 we clambered up the enormous steps of the Pyramide del Sol - Mexico City radiating across the plain, dull mountains and smoke from the factories...

According to the Hopi, all the native peoples of the American continent were brought into this, the 4th World, through an omphalos, a navel, in the Colorado riverbed. They set out on their eight great rotational migratory paths, returning after an endless time to the world-focus at Four Corners, Arizona. Every civilization in America was a spin-off from this orbiting - the planets of the Inca and the Sioux alike were rooted in this selfsame sun.

"Migration, like reproduction, is part of the life-cycle, and depends upon a complex internal rhythm that affects the whole organism, particularly the endocrine glands and the gonads." Sometimes at night I walk out of the front door and cross the street to the sea-wall for a breath of fresh air. The tall cranes and the lightstrings of the now largely defunct docks are off to the left, while away in the West the slim red sliver of the new moon hangs in the sky.

*

Lights of your city. Washed with rain.

The density of Earth. The lost eye of

Women from your eyes. Men from your eyes.

*

(the vessel speaks)

I am too beautiful to be here
I am unpronounceable

You've met me before somewhere?
I am too beautiful
red antlers   our songs
sprout from the top of my head
                        are arrived here
                from within heaven they come
my home is a glass cube
I am easily broken

My numbers are knotted in the calendar
my bones are the bones of lost animals

When I ask your purpose
                you stop my mouth
I shovel speech into yours
        like wet sand

You've seen my belly reflected in the golden windows of the Chase
                        Manhattan Bank
you've pulled my elbow out of the mud at Passchendaele
I am not an Aztec
I am too old for that

I am not from a distant star
I am too old for that
my eyes don't care
you walking round and round like dogs

Your eyes don't see a distant star
remember when you ransacked my grave?
you came too close to home

You are a head sticking out from a wall
do you know where that temple is?
You have been there before

I am not Maya
(but you are too young to know)
your eyes are wet clay

You are the last rung in a long ladder
we are sitting on the edge of the Moon's blade
I am a white line engraved in high gravel
I am a wildcat, and share faces with the god of
                                        your choice

                    *

Thursday afternoon. From the library reference room you can hear the ranter at work in the muggy street below: "So it is said that in Christ, and through the power alone of Christ Jesus, it is ye are reborn." The pedestrian precinct works a strict perspective and the evangelist's voice is propelled to vanishing point. "And if ye be not born...and if ye be not re-born..." he should go on - "the Word will vanish! And then ye shall drown in eternity, the bucket of desire, for IT, the One Word!"

The story goes that once upon a time there was a tongue to women, men and animals, laced with fuse-wire, gold, 'the true 'tree of life within my own mouth' as I-Jahman sings, which is also the inter-dependence of species - the Siberian Yakut with their wild reindeer herds, piss-drinkers alike for precious salts and secondhand amanita chemicals.

See the scurrying crowd of office workers and shoppers reflected in silver windows. No bone-words now for the job, no quetzalfeather words. Why, all the names could be changed in an instant, and a single keyword propel us to vanishing point!

And it is said that migrants often return to the exact place where they were hatched, a journey sometimes covering thousands of miles and years. Topographical and climactic landmarks are used: coastlines, deserts, river-systems, ice-packs, air-currents, temperature masses, as well as celestial bearings. Genetic maps.

So I put this down from out of those gracious pots — animal and human faces intermingled, animal heads on human bodies, faces, muscles, limbs. Later I write some elaborate lines called 'riddles' which whittle down to 'the vessel speaks'. The pots then ask me if I think I speak on their behalf? Do I presume that psilocybe alone is enough to pour myself out as hollow and clean as they are?

But actually, they are silent and fragile and motionless, staring out to an endless present.

*

(the vessel speaks)

What am I?
my head is shiny
    clean red clay

            my thigh
        dyed with a cream spiral
                    hunches beneath my belly

my heart is light

            I am chewing coca-leaves
        with my hands on my knees
                Fire burn hot! Fire burn cold!
                    my bones are the bones of lost animals

    You are the red vein. The seed moves inside you
like the clear white letters of a text, a text to which
the gun-priest is deaf, dumb and blind.

The outline of this city is that of a giant cat.
The day of its release has long been knotted in the calendar.

Lime-leaves scatter through the windy avenues
of this silent, crawling place. Who are you?

I am a white line engraved in high gravel
   my date is knotted in music

                        lake-isle
                              drifts like a bird
                        in the ice-blue

         Who am I?
            I am your true love
            I am your gourd

                        *

*So little is known about those first migrations, the words scattering across
the globe, genesis succeeding genesis in the returning wind.*

*Me, you, we, them - the subjection of the subject I thought, peering down
into the little glass cases.*

*They stare out into a future that may be the only one that can preserve
them: devolution to bio-region, an almost inconceivably long stride, we are
so far buried beneath our tongues.*

*They question their own calendar, and what it has predicted for us. They
interrogate every word of our future histories.*

                        *

"Come, 'Prince of the Flowers'
put down your white roots to my eye

the Earth is our body
the dark grass
that stretches away to the 4 Winds

in bones yes! of silver
we take our
of copper
delight

'*con nuestros flores*'
take delight

put down your bed in this sweet-pine delta

sweet republic"

*

Bronzes

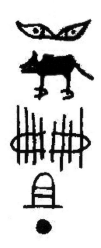

Aubade

Violet dawn
and to all who work in its weakest light
tidings, the sweepers in doorways,
ID checkers,
waking in flung cities

man on the roadway
broad straw brush, straw-hatted
and you,
below my window,
whipping your horse

foreigners falling
out of the sky
onto swollen streets
whipped by the dawn

and to all those millions
camped by the station
to go

who've given shape
and furrowed the heart,
who build, and who destroy,
your factories, gates and walls

cough in its light,
who walk,
repairers of cities,
woken

Against The Wall

Mao said:
all who journey
to the Great Wall
should be called "heroes",
"true men".

A father to his son:
"Now you're a real hero!"
An entire nation of heroes! –
more and more tourists,
better transport, *food* ! –
now anyone can get here.

Bought a Great Wall medal
from the souvenir shop –
now *I'm* a hero.

"Actually, Nixon did a lot of good for the Chinese people,
            he helped to open the door..."

   It was built to keep out the *Xiung-Nu*
"but it doesn't mean much in modern warfare!"
and Liu laughed.
"Look at the graffiti!" he cried,
pointing at the mass of neatly-chiselled characters
in the clean new stone –
   "they all want to be – immortal!"

(Liu had been "sent to the countryside")

The 18 Arhants of Canyan Shan

cang   yan   shan

blue   rock   mountain

redder than blue
well into Autumn
        broad yellow maple leaves
    drift through the damp air

    alone in the mist
            with the ghosts of Canyan
        brightly painted arhants
        (climb the long staircase)

            struggling for ever
                    with their tigers
                or their hungers,
                    stretching out their arms
                        — embracing the mountain

in a dry, hard land
    the old river-bed
        is valuable: broad and flat

    — a girl in a pink headscarf
            carries another bucket of stones
        from the greening field —

whatever they mine here
        is near the surface —

big pink holes in the ground
and most of it by hand

"but the feelings of the people
(Xiao Yi tells me)
run very deep"

*

What is the meaning of this?
The moon rests on an upraised
palm
— a brightly painted bird
that refuses to fly away

more red than blue
the stones of the streambed —
Princess Nanyang came here
and cut off all her hair
renouncing the world

'and her tears streaked the stones'

Princess Nanyang
cut off her hair
— and renounced the war

she wept
— streaking the pebbles

this is Expounding Rock
and behind this curtain is where she slept

it is very cold, there are birds in
the fog

ten musicians
escort her statue, smiling
with clappers and fingers raised
above drums and invisible strings

there is no music
but our own voices
the shuffling of boots
on cold stone

Shandong

You know what
rain is? Rain
is green, the sea says,
rain is sleep, she
cross your mind with silver
says, you
know what sand is?
Sand is towns
and forest
pulverised to gold

your palm with soldiers
cross the land
says I am shiny,
black
we'll rise together
says, and I will burn
beneath your feet
and I will sweat
beneath your hands

and Ice?
is elsewhere –
opium years dug into the ground
– the pushers' bones say
Ice
is nowhere,
plastic sheeting
covers the furrows,
dazzles, sweats
the seedlings
sleeping
yet

The Kunming Train

We wish that we could plunge
into this landscape like a train
into a mountain, snake
to orange ground, for miles
from heat, the press of circum –
stances. Coal-dust grimes our faces,
pages rustle in the wind.
An open window – reek
of coal and night-soil.
Towns give way repeatedly
to blood-pink ground
and water-buffalo, splashing
crystals into the bright air.
The power's everywhere –
they've got the electricity
about all right – it spans the mountains,
valleys, broad enough
to hold a hundred little towns.
A dozen sampans
sleeping on the river.
Freight trains
sweating coal.
The act of composition –
of this land, the
transformation
of the Chinese earth.
All day this train weaves in and out of tunnels.
There she stands, in black,
a basketful of greens,
her buckled face,
and green
the contours of her life.
Right up along the tracks
the ground is thick
with cabbages and corn.

Yunnan: we listen to the radio,
a stranger song, drink smokey tea.
A woman on the street
is selling beetles from a lunch-box–
churn the earth, improve
the earth.

The hats the women wear
are woven cane, in cones –
the banding radiates and splits
from point to brim, as weaving
bands the pinnacle of Heaven to the Earth –
the characters you write, the mountains that you
write –
the clouds
roll back into the sun
and plunge to one another
blue and orange.
Chance
is married to necessity
of harvest, pregnancy and money.
So, the gods are kind
or angry,
nations also.
So, the oldest faith of all
is worshipping the ancestors,
burning money in secret,
spinning money, changing
money, in the cafe –
things there are that only other
money buys, a whiff
of other worlds
along the edges of the tracks
where children wave,
imagine cities
that they're said to have inherited.

The train arrives.

The platform hovers under our feet.

"the valley so deep
and the mountains so high
that the people there thought
that was all that there was
                        to the sky"

*

An old woman
whose eyes are like clocks
on a dusty building,
telephone wires hanging in grey air,
fixed with the speech inside her

*

At night, lorries
and mules trundle on
Weijing Lu. Oily lights
in the noodle-houses,
whip-cracks, the wind
rattling flags,
twisting the smoke
from the coal-stoves.
One fat cook in a dirty apron,
her face polished by steam.
The mules persist, haul cabbages,
or an impossible pile of bricks.

*

The moon on a dirty canal
says a lot in this city

The Book of Hills and Seas

If this were a world of new corn,
if this were a world of mountain mists,
I could lie back, and take it slow,
sing my songs with steady feet,
plough that furrow.

Then I could direct my mind
to the true,
the true proportion of my house.

Alas when I cross the canal,
alas when I walk the street,
when I pick up the town
my hands get crossed,
when I pick up the book of the town
the air is thick –

Tao Chien, please
open for me
your Book of Hills and Seas!

Big Drum

Xi Ha Da Gu
the sky's
a yellow
drum

Xi Ha Da Gu
the field
a loaded gun

for now's the time
    to eat the sun
to bring it in, to stack the yards –
the past remains an endless field
    of blood and shit and stone,
tomorrow is the Song of Songs
    but now's the time to bring the harvest home

The Bell

I heard 150 different sorts of food mentioned
in one song –
this is the Song of Songs!
the Hundred-Headed Sunflower!

Gunmetal ground, it is
piss, blood, smoke.
Money is burnt in secret
to feed the ancestors

blood, stone, maize.
White
statues of warriors, beasts,
the length of the Sacred Way,
the Earth so old
    it rings like a bell.

People filling the fields
in pink, brown and blue.
The wind is warm, shaking
the fat persimmons.
Big green lorries
blow through the villages.

Lao Shan

(Old Mountain)

Here
the Earth twirls
like a fish
the mountain's rhythms
rock-face, smoothed by wind,
firs, the saw-tooth ridges
ripping the sky
and terraces, bent to the slopes
   – the bow-curve's strength,
the *'feng-shui'*,
'wind and water'

             where
a boulder, slit like a one-thousand-year-old egg
cut deep
cut red
the characters
there, the creation
there, the lightning-sword

that woman
bent on her hoe,
she's so straight-backed
from pulling that bow –
the walls, the tunnels,
the farms

           wrapping the mountain
             staunching the flow to ground
               of its
            precious crown

A Lohan

Under a thick Saturday sky,
villages scrabbled of brown brick,
tunnels, arches,
threaded in yellow stone
we see –
two women with chestnut heads,
a bent mule and a cartful of corn-cobs:
capsules of vivid light.

        See
the earth, shelved, squeezing seeds
to juice, a coat of winter wheat,
the mountain.
        See
the cave, the cold
colours,
        the bodhisattva,
picking his ear,

        thinking
What's the sky up to?
A thousand floods
they come and go
there's something got stuck in my ear –
they come they go,
feet, water, blood.
In Liaoning Province they've dug up a skeleton,
Homo Erectus – 200,000
years old
– there's something got stuck in my ear –
the species achieved
an upright posture in motion
developed the use of stone tools –

        he wonders
      what's the sky doing?

rocking
back and forth
and see
the silhouettes of men in helmets
working on a gantry,
donkey
pulling a pile of ancient straw.

Snowfall

We think of this dirty old city
gone white: the star on the tower,
footprints in snow between her door and mine.

No chance – it will melt as it falls
and the streets will be brown streaks.
She catches buses and stares at the sky,
there are piles of cabbages everywhere.

Writing to lovers in distant cities,
there there is warmth and light and food.
Walnuts and a red candle,
touching the backs of each other's hands.

There, there's a world made simple
as snow, when the sun vibrates in the trees,
and as complex as Winter, when everyone
shudders and rushes
        in shivering cities.

New Year Train

Fireworks flare
the length of the night,
terraces, rivers,
curl

the Ox-year:
    'shoulder
    to
    the
    grindstone'

dimly-lit, a
smoky carriage,
irritable *fu-yuans*,
those who must work
and have places to go
my only companions

drink!
to this then –
the flower of food
opens red
in the stomach of China

'yi bai sui'

(a 100-year-old man)

5 green hills
    at Wu Tai Shan –
the slopes and terraces of mind

    below us
          roads and farms,
    around us
          mountains

        Where are the seers?
        Where are the blind?

     His hands are rhymes
       of dust and trees
      that ring and ring again
          until the bell of the earth cracks
         and his eyes close
           to light and pain

the time is chiming in Beijing
    while thousands wait
      to board their trains –
no sound,
   no colour,
     nothing that's oblivious to heat and rain
    can thrust or scatter
              time
   means all and nothing to this place

    His senses five are rhythms that
    the world has written in his face.

Forest of Stelae

Border guards
reach for the lone-star
stations of cold
dust
at the Western Gate

jet-fighter
wrapped in a tarp
bells
register
noon wind

Xi'an –
your walls
beg questions – their mass
undoes me
quite

flags
stretch for the wind-star
stations
of cold
light

tell me
to hold my ground
here on this gate
behold
this fearful industrial freight

*

The gods of the town
ring
in Shang bronze

– *shang* –

'almost as if
a fear of space'
design
drenching the bronze

spear-head –
grace
of its edge

smoke over the town

*

Stretch
for the sky
like a leaf
or a stone
eyeless
and glazeless
halfborn
the sky
matted

flags, bells
reach for the star

halfborn regiments
shivering horse-ass
sunk in rock-sun

headless
star-baked
sleepwalkers

ranks, grooves,
one
squat on his knee
stalking towards a wall
of 20th century light

*

Eternal surfacing —
jump-jet
wrapped in a tarp

bells, border-guards
reach for the night
at the wide gate

*

Hexagram 56. The Wanderer

fire spreads   strange lands
                                   & separation

seeking new fuel   home/
                     is the road

"Grace = fire, breaking out from the secret
                depths of the Earth"

— beauty of form

— heavenly form — the sun & heavenly bodies

— time, & changing demands

love = inner content

justice = the changing form

*

Notes:

Tao Chien *(365–427* A.D.) otherwise known as Tao Yuan Ming, one of China's greatest nature poets, renowned as a recluse.

Xi Ha Da Gu the name of a local opera tradition (Xi Ha Big Drum).

lohan a monk. The poem refers again to Can Yan Shan in Hebei Province. Here, in a temple built astride a deep chasm, is a collection of brightly-painted, life-size statues of Buddhist monks in a hilarious variety of attitudes: drinking, tugging their long white eyebrows, rolling their fat white bellies, "struggling with their tigers". Such congregations can be found elsewhere in China (notably in the Bamboo Temple near Kunming) and together constitute a little-known masterpiece of Buddhist comic art.

Xi'an ('Western Peace') ancient capital, now an industrial sprawl, well known for the nearby terracotta army of the tyrant Qin Shi Huang Di who unified China through ruthless means and was also responsible for the building of the Great Wall.

Wu Tai Shan a major Buddhist temple complex in Shanxi Province.

fu-yuans general term for maids and female public employees e.g. train stewardesses.

arhant one who seeks, finds and dwells in Nirvana.

Two Incarnations

(*Tu Fu*) In The Cities

Sharing the same couch, chatter to each other as they drink
I come here in search of an elixir
phantom zones as of big rivers crossing
prepared for which life this time?

the clattering of futures is hard to hear him over
who speaks of justice when heaven casts its net?
late Autumn on Mt. Tai, the river flowing east
falling through fog of time-rivers crossing

and the incessant plains, and I know the Emperor
waging incessant war on his frontiers
and I am a ghost, and I know that I can't be heard over
                    the incessant clamouring of futures
like dealers I was old before my time

shook up like dice in a cup
dice on the swampy monstrous plains thrown out
and up to the frontiers old men, and I am what you might say
shanghaied, and carried away in a little boat in my heart
                              and know nothing

the waves break in the Milky Way,
bottles of burning, shuddering in the capsule street
my ancient love shudders in the fracture between zones
waves of violence crashing about me, bridges, canals of my
                    cities up-rising

Yellow River switches away to the cities
stars pop out of their sockets, their grid-reference
I is a figure of speech inverted the masses shiver and stand up
ceaseless the rain and my stitched coat collapsing

money is hard and bright to come by a naked state
fires and beacon-fires city to mud-ridden city multiply
dolor and mud stepping out for my wine-ration
final coins and the land is forgotten and lost in clouds

my wife and children I am unemployed for forty years
insurrected streets the city of old brocade
a nation ought to know its boundaries
daggers and honey-tongues night of rebellion night

farmland astoundingly generous, patient and pregnant
peasants dragged off to the lines for thousands consecutive
                                                    sentences
this a poor house with only stale wine for a bottle
I wish that the pines would spring for a thousand feet

*

In these my cities muddy paths the 4 Oceans bending and
                                                    ceasing
in farmland incessant swampy immobile fog-washed the hills
                                            chanting
wine-drunk the old days with Li Bai god among poets
sharing the same couch, jug-sweat, ancient love

my thatched roof is destroyed by the Autumn wind
1966-76 a great sunburst of political ecstasy
broken glass and broken the knees of the righteous war
rain on my hands and the dealers flutter the god-pictures

wind on my neck in the days the nights of up-rising
thousands the poems the years sloshing from dung-carts
English the cities and I am a ghost and I know that I am
                                        a deafness
i.e. I am unheard, and unknown, but by myself I am
                            thoroughly known

as a phoenix rising from vortex to vortex
watching the gutter with wine snaring the stomach
one luxurious plant in the park and flowers of cold coins
the rich and the wretched chattering, rayon meat tin and
                                                            futures

characters turn and the meaning rises and stands up
as hills in fog, meaning, only the hills and streams remain
and I write nothing, boat in my heart chanting
the river flows, fraction of brush and paper

                              *

Tu Fu in search of elixir-time by-passing
Monument, Bank, over London Bridge so many
placebo-river, switching away to the border
I wish that the pines would spring a thousand feet

I is a figure of speech encradled
name on a mountain of thought a fiction
I is a fiction a true chanting
time that is crashing a coat collapsing

pines a thousand feet to wish up-springing
poem a thousand children thousand pronoun
thousand years bamboo growing human heart a similar song
the ghosts are lonely lovely time-rivers crossing
earth the gift the mountain-cities creaking

*

Ruan Ji's Island

Starfish and bunkers extend in the sand,
sand and forgetful grass sprawl the hilltop.
The chambers break open the placenames escape from their
prisons,
the chambers break, and the codes of the sand and the fish
are released,
the ciphers of birdnames, and baynames, and nameless
waves.
I've waited for this moment – now I come, on horseback, flying,
– such are the rocks!

The courtyards broke, and the waves and rocks rode
flooding, in,
the blue-white tide of time-flowers opened.
Blown through crags, the gannets, thousands pouring –
blown through crags and colonies of time and light.
Extending the sand I walk the hilltop,
stand, my heart like a violet, raising my head in forgetful grass.

I'm waiting for this moment, riding beaches,
eyeing the rising moon and seanames curling.
Who can know me, know my anxiety,
flooding the turrets over a thousand years?
Red-beaked birds react like swords to the flood that turns
about me,
heart like gorse-petals, gifting a coconut scent on the wind.

Who can know me, code of grass and cuttleshell?
Which road can you take to find me, heart like ashes, body like
withered trees?
The sand-road, west of the airfield, zig-zag down the cliffs,
the pebble-road, built by slaves to the fort.
Which road can you tread towards my joy?
The rocks fold over, the seawaves fall to the sky.

None the road to take you far, I watch the forts and houses
                              rise and fall,
the garrisons and guns, the codes of withered trees.
The words the only things that know me,
red-beaked oystercatcher's current cut against the wind,
the boats that drift along the current into land.
And commerce flowers, fades, my clothes transmute,

the clouds accelerate. Villains, bureaucrats,
scratch their codes in the sand and me my songs.
Grass grows up all over forgotten invasions,
I translate it: nations' roads lead nowhere,
sea's elixir flushes them from the hill.

The Yellow Sparrow thought that it had no predators.
The sea's no predators, the rocks its prey,
the cliffs already sand, the sea's forgetting.
Armies come and go, the sun and moon stare into each
                              other's eyes.
Thin and as pale as a ghost I walk the beach, mumbling and
                              chanting
I write this poem – which way will you take to find my joy?

The road runs north and south, the road runs east and west –
which way will you take to find me written? Name to use?
Which dynasty to serve me? Horse to ride?
The sun and moon stare into each other's eyes.

So Kuafu's stick became the Forest of Deng?
The grass and the herring-gull squirl in a single shell!
The tracks of the wind and the seaweed, listen,
are mine, the sand-voice, treading the beach,
and poor my clothing, gladly.

Even the words of the gods and the goddesses cannot be
                                        trusted –
the seawaves shred on the breakwater, jewellery,
ships of commerce rock on the tides of trade and history,
teartracks cross my face, the wind is in my eyes.
I wear only humble clothes to tread the cliffs
as lightbeams cross me – four from one side,
five from the other – jewellery breaks and dissolves...

Yin and Yang are a paintbox: oystercatchers black and white
                        of back and wing,
tiny forget-me-not, blue, with microscopic sun in head,
invisible rabbits in thousands of underground palaces!
Sunstreams, moonstreams. Who says the Way is not to be seen?

Mannez is a hundred yards of stone no more.
In Marais Square a blood-red heart on a pub, and hands in
                                emblem, joined and ciphered.
A horse, when I come, reacts in his paddock to ripples in air.
A crab and a cairn on the money, tilted rocks with a time-ripple
                                through them.
The way to discover me: rippling and riding through language
                                                of space.

Thus I transform, translate. I hear the cliffs and the concrete.
My life is translated, and this is eternal,
talking in ciphers, freely, beyond comprehension.
The sea's edge breaks and ripples, the tide, in its rising and
                                 falling, demolishes certainty.
Coming and going the stars to steer by. Write it – it is so.

All the old dynasties breaking, one remains:
birdheart and flower unfolding,
characters written. I ride the cliffs in calligraphy,
see all folk, the first spring bee, and break in laughing.
The salt-water cipher of zero releases the emerald wave that
                            breaks and splinters,
                                blooming into eternal sky.

*

Alderney
March 1989

For My Father

At first, little outcrops were quarried.

Small industries developed.

Coal began to be used instead of charcoal to smelt iron.

Steam,

canals, replacing packhorses.

Simultaneously, the enclosures took place; the peasants, already weakened by agricultural depression, flooded into the new industrial areas. Early photographs show pigs and poultry scrabbling around the walls of what really amount to little smallholdings, cobbled together in alleyways and streets; women wearing leather aprons, girls in smocks and broad-brimmed hats.

Coal: there were 3 major faults underlying the area; the southern band, Dudley and Clent, was a 30ft.-thick seam, extremely rich in iron ore. 'Wenlock' or 'Dudley' limestone, known as 'crog-balls', was a greenish limestone which looked like lenses, formed from masses of the skeletons of tiny 'life-forming organisms'.

*

As my father's short-term memory fades, his recall of long-ago events increases in brilliance. He lives for a moment in a football game, played on an old potato-field and they used to run dogs and hunt rabbits there; barrels of pickles in my grandmother's grocery shop and rabbits hanging from the ceiling.

"Florrie! Florrie!" (who was Florrie?) he shouts from his hospital chair.

"They'd better watch out for that railway line. It's alright now but it's going to subside..."

*

Quarrying: bone-lime-ridges, stretching above the Midland Plain, dividing the watersheds of the Trent and Severn; this is the foundation stone of industrial Britain. And fireclay: Stourbridge, Quarry Bank, Brierley Hill and Lye, producing the finest glass in the world. Upper Gornal and Gornal Wood made 'incomparable' furnace-linings.

One of the furthest points from the sea in the whole of Britain, yet here the heaviest anchors were forged as well as lighthouse lamps and boilers for ships.

Elihu Burnett, US Consul to Birmingham, wrote in 1869, after standing on Dudley Castle Hill at night:

  "The sublimest battle-scenes ever enacted on earth; ten thousand Titans were essaying to breach heaven with a thousand mortars, each charged with a small red-hot hill."

*

Words are never metal, never blood. He's sleeping, 'silent as a baby', fatter now than he has been. Bright new blood comes into his cheeks with a memory or an action, the squeeze of a hand. A warm hand, and somewhere inside himself he sweeps the leaves aside, of blood and metal, money or brick. He mutters a house, he murmurs a railway line, subsiding. Metal of money, erections. Leaves of factories, night-shifts, days and men.

You notice the old on the streets like never before, the ailments and the qualities of everyone – he's overweight, she's overanxious, she has a terrible limp. You listen to neighbourly gossip of kidneys, or the transplant of a vein from heart to leg. And this is the Dragon Year - a train crash, a plane bombing. Where is the Self, which voice of this dying man?

Leaves round the roots of trees, like leather, or stained glass crimson, but never like blood.

The fresh blood of the leaves that blow in his head. Gone now is the talking pain and the skull under document skin. No little jokes to make him smile, nor any recognitions. Now he's private, cleaning his karma, wiping the tapes, cathecting.

In Baggeridge Woods an ancient beech, shattered and blackened, is still, compared to others, a sprig - the whole thing creaking, hanging there on the wind and the sharpened sun. Some scripts are cut in its bright green side, say "1917" and "M&J": signatures, expanding and dissolving in the century's swell; ripples and scripts of its growth.

The body is full of tunnels, fossils and paintings. I was born on the edge of a quarry, 'the Wren's Nest', a limestone escarpment with council-houses, tilting now and cracking, labyrinth of fleshlight.

Dad you are on the edge now, the edge of not-being.

*

Come into the circle, let me help you find the words, help you to spell.

Tell me about the photos, you in your suit with the wide lapels and Oxford bags on holiday, arm in arm with Mom. Yes, very fashionable! What was the love like?

Tell me, what was it like when you lifted the plane? It was heavy oblong lump of ash and steel. You'd lift it up by the shiny dark red, well-palmed handle, your eyes steady above the vice, then swing it down. The oiled and certain blade would whisper the pine away in fragrant curls. I never had your hand for this kind of thing Dad, I pushed it away. You wanted, you expected I suppose, me to take you up on it. Well, if it's not too obvious, I try to do the same with words instead, to make a table or chair that will take the weight.

Tell me what was *your* Dad like? Why did you never talk about him? But then, you never talked about anyone. What *did* you talk about? "Greece? A bloody awful place to fight a war." The best times were happily silent, waiting by the canal for the half-pound chub to pounce!

*

Creatures sift in the weight of brine and sludge, dying to make a world. Faces torched the sweat-shops. Cut in the bark of factory-walls, deserted, the names of women and men whose ore and grease produced the country.

Tell me father –

I remember – men on buses smoking Woodbines, greasy knap-sacks, freezing roads to factories on night-shifts –

you remember Greece – that woman, standing in a doorway – what a bloody awful place to fight a war – the dogs – remember Flor-rie - days and nights of scarlet fever – you were only two – they'd bet-ter watch that bridge – and dressed in black she was – and beautiful –
*

Remember him in his shed, we sawed asbestos together, I held it. He built the shed and the garage himself, cupboards, fireplaces, shelves. His joints were perfect. Nothing but perfect would do. He had beautiful tools for the job.

I'd like to say that Gornal town is a sort of iron rose
         that's forged by all the men of this vicinity
         – it's in their blood, to saw, to carve, to work in flame –
         an emblem cast from solid craft and common cause –

                    but no –
         one day he died.

         We walk around in speech-marks,
                  and there is no edge, to town or face, to claim
                                        or fall from.

         As I type, the threat of demolition fades –
            these lines are strewn across a disused factory wall,

         its light is lake-like, massive, and there is no weight.

                              *

After Gododdin

I

Some verses grew like a tree
from a red-wet field —

its leaves flicker: "this is the Gododdin, sung by Aneirin":

        the Stone-White Book of the Dead,
        the Red-Green Book of the Living,
        the Piss-Hide Book of War.

This is the bloody Gododdin, "sung by Aneirin".

                 *

Eidyn =
Edinburgh.

What was a 'city' then?
Where stood the fort of the Gododdin?
Those heroes strode was it
here?
where a squall runs past us up the old volcano's side
and a bee is hanging
soft,
black-legged,
dead,
in a thorn-bush,
bright as the loch below is reflective
as any gap in a manuscript?

Roads like armour-straps wrap
and sparrows buckle from post to wire
shop-rooves of Catraeth, now Catterick,
sung as:

                the Snow-Marble Book of the Martyrs,
                the Grass-Gold Book of Survival.

Aneirin slipped the leash
to spurt through the crags of available language,
a coarse and glistening grain,
to chant the heroes,
those, who with their shoulder-companions
died at Catraeth;
those feather-hearted thugs
who ravens thanked for filling their beaks
and eagles thanked,
yet are now just brooches of cloud-shadow
over a sloping field
in wolf-shape,
ox-shape,
sea-horse,
stag –

whose signatures are buried deep under stones and streets.

From Eidyn to Catraeth
the only tribute to these slain
Aneirin 's –
leaves that fall today like sun
in elegiac rain.

                        *

2

(Coigach and Loch Assynt, Sutherland)

The gauntleted hand of a mountain sticks straight up into the wind, a shower of spears: Stac Pollaidh. It is a reaper, a combative eagle. The land below is a tatter of lochs and trackless hills, a page from a manuscript shredded by time-claws. The trees of Inverpolly, thousands of feet below, are indistinguishable: these are the mere men who were dragged along for the fray.

Of 300 'hounds' or knights, with indeterminate retinues, none escaped but one, Aneirin. None but the bard. "Though the army drank bright mead by the light of their tapers, the bitterness lasted long; on Sunday the blades were distributed, on Monday streams of blood ran down their knees."

"In this there is no variant."

300. Plus how many thousand more? They earned this clarified mead which we swallow by battery-light in the caravan at Achnahaird. Tonight I'm kept awake for them, working a kind of crown to bind the hills - the skulls of Suilven, Canisp, Quinag, outlined under starlight.

   "*Crugyn* – a slab of rock in a cleared land, a flood in every
lowland –

                    Cadfannan – with the swoop of an eagle across the
mouth of a river –

             Urfai – swift on the tracks of the deer –

                              Cynwal – he glutted
the grasp of the eagles' beaks –

                         Merin – he was a grave, a bloodbath
of dark-coloured hawks –

Isag – whose
manners were like the sea-flood, gracious, his pleasant drinking
of mead –

Gwadnerth –
who defended the mead and the cornfields of Gododdin from the
mongrel hosts of England, nourished on wine –

Cynwal – taking up his spear, his scarlet reaper, as if it were
sparkling wine in vessels of glass –

Gwarddur – gave out presents from his winter
horsehoard..."

*

Where I live, in Edinburgh, Milton Street is a canyon of tenements,
once a slum, at the end of which is a gate into Holyrood Park – the
happy hunting ground at one time for the palace gentry, visiting
royals. I can see their lackeys creaking open the heavy black gate on
special days for the smoke-choked populace to bathe in sunshine,
stretch their legs.

The wind is buffeting the caravan and I sing this for the mongrels,
nameless as they are, by torchlight, meadlight. Theirs the available
language, written in the gaps where ancient manuscripts are punctured, filling in the margins where they're glued and overlapped.

*

"Men went to Catraeth.
They were the sea-flood, they were meat for eagles,
for the cattle-herds, the sweet yellow mead.

Men went to Catraeth.
They were ravens, showers of spears
for cattle-herds, intoxicating mead.

Men rode to Catraeth.
They were ravens in the green dawn
for the cattle, the sweet wine, and mead.

Men rode to Catraeth.
They were wolves, they were golden torques
for the cornfields, for the yellow mead.

Men went to Catraeth
and none came back
but I, Aneirin,
none but I, as Taliesin knows.

None from Catraeth.
They were wine-coloured hawks, they were graves
for Eidyn, the bee-yellow mead.

Men rode to Catraeth.
Spear-showers, palisades of alder
for the horse-hoards and the mead.

Men to Catraeth
and none returning.
They were brooches.
None but Aneirin, for the sake of his brilliant poetry –
earning his bee-wine,
    sunbright
      sweet,
        intoxicating mead."

                    *

3

Memory rots,
leaves gaps of punctuation,

empty quotation marks.
Others fill them in with lullabies,
love-songs, descriptions of snowy landscapes.
Even today, in the park,
could be the time where one of them fell.

*

Picts, Britons, Celts,
they all "fell".
I wanted to turn the original dirge around,
but there isn't one.
"I am dead" says Aneirin, "and never lived."

*

It's said there was no true Celtic epic:
more so than anywhere else in Europe
the poet's role was to buttress the aristocracy.
Even now we're afraid to go off the road
and camp where there isn't a site!

*

Memory's a tract of land
that's punctured, punctuated.
Coigach's rocky coast, colloided,
pours into the sea,
the ancient warfares still to be expunged.

*

Scotland is nearly devoid of forest –
let the mongrels return as trees
to populate the land!

*

As it grows
the poem dwindles -
more and more paper gets thrown away.

*

The poem is thrown on a wheel
and worn away. This
is a geological metaphor.
So are we all.

*

The battle-grounds are ploughed beneath a map.

*

The poem is haunted by something that actually happened.

*

The Art of War

"Ku"   Work on What Has Been Spoiled

'the character represents a bowl in whose contents worms are breeding'

> — it is not ours, but it is our interest /
> it is not a border, yet it is a border

Birds fly in a cloud across a Lanarkshire housing estate - evening and morning I see them from the train to work. Our soldiers, south in the desert several thousand miles, have today achieved a momentous victory. Rubbish lies in heaps along the tracks, through out-of-work town after town.

'What has been spoiled through human fault can be made again through human work. It is not immutable fate. Work towards improving human conditions promises well. It accords with the time.'

On we go, from station to station. A woman gets on in a shabby anorak with two or three kids in tow. She is on her way to Glasgow to stake a claim. The train fare isn't cheap.

All over town there are people writing stories, poems, history, lives. It may never be seen in print, but nevertheless it *is* written.

Warfare:

> it is ours, yet it is not /
> right and justice, might and technology

> strength and will: it is market rhetoric /

blanket rhetoric, daily censorship

might and technology, history in the making

friendly fire
halfway round / a small world

*

"Shih"   The Army

'6 in the 3rd place means: Perchance the army carries corpses in the wagon. This is quite without merit and bodes severe defeat. The hexagram stresses discipline and control.

The military strength of a nation lies in the masses of its people. If the bottom lines of the hexagram change, the lower trigram becomes Tui, 'Joyfulness', whereby order is upset, for joyousness is not the proper frame of mind for the onset of war.

Three changing lines are sufficient to move the hexagram to Sun, 'the Gentle Penetrating Wind, or Tree Roots'.

a handful of gravel towards their monument
it is, thousands of seeds in a handful of mud

it's a traffic-jam full of bodies, terrible weather
deafness, foxholes, friendly fire

it is rupturing supply-lines, it is over-simplification
it is satellites, what I am told

it is, freedom of speech, it is somewhere else
the newspapers ignite with sympathy,

the friendly fire of rhetoric, dictatorship
heads on stakes, no music, blown disguise

it's a hundred years of 50,000 men to build a wall
the capital, the flag, the leader's photo warts and all

a beautifully-worked triangular dagger-blade,
a gas, a piece of wood, a boot, a wire,
                anything that's to hand

deaf-music, tinsel glittering through radars,
broadcasts baffled by dunes and banks

windpipes snaffled by burnt-out transport
throats that are blocked by bones

it is reparations / no it is not reparations /
it is flags and standards / the brighter the colour,
                the stronger the camouflage

the day of battle a day like any other,
a night, a Tuesday afternoon, this place
                like any other —

                        *

'It disperses clouds'

Clarity and judgement which thwarts all dark and hidden motives,
bringing secret influences to light, thus causing them to lose their power
over people.

'Penetration should be affected not by an act of violation but by an influence
that never lapses.'

                        *

monument

(from a sculpture by Rob Kennedy)

They were farmers,
they grew vegetables.

In bad years, their vegetables were black,
in good years, they were white and green and as firm
as muscle.

Marathon
Salamis
Leuctra
Cynocephali

They grew meat.

In bad years, the meat was stringy, the texture
of emery paper. In good years, they smoked it, and in Winter
watered their throats with its salt.

Catraeth
Passchendaele
Dien Ben Phu

They were farmers,
and grew soil.

In bad years, they grew dust and wrote their quivering
letters in it. In good years you couldn't even see the soil,
so thick their work.

Kuwait
Hong Kong
Los Angeles

They were farmers, meteorologists, and therefore prophets,
They had to be. They always knew what was coming.
They grew the past like muscle. The ground was slippery
with blood and cannon-grooves.
Their dykes were ripped
and their houses were built with fire.
Their thin glass veins were flooded with morphine.

This is a handful of gravel towards their monument.

*

from: 1001 Things To Ask Of Any City

236.   How many bricks are there in that chimney, that massive red cinema wall? Who made those bricks? What pressure can they stand, the ones who made those bricks?

237.   Calculate the income of the biggest house within a stone's throw of your own and relate it to the financial assets of a friend who lives on SS in a B&B with a couple of kids, an anorak and an electric fire.

238.   Go back to that biggest house. How many of the smallest houses would fit in the biggest house?

239.   Have you heard the one about the poodle in the microwave? What about the tortoise in the tumble-drier?

*

323.   Do you realize that every bridge in your city is a bridge of sighs?

325.   How many birds nest under the asthma viaducts?

326.   Is your city surrounded?

327.   How many calories could you find in the average dustbin?

328.   How many bottles of Thorazine are drunk every day in your city?

329.   Why can't you answer my questions, walls?

*

494. How would you feel if everybody laughed out loud at the very same moment?

495. If all the graffiti were written out loud, would they then be as long as Genesis?

496. And all that "writing on the wall" - what does it tell you about the next ten minutes?

497. On all the oak-trees within your city - are there as many leaves as there are eyes of the populace?

498. Is your city a walled city?

499. In which part of town do all the magistrates live?

*

633. So why didn't you think to ask these questions before?

636. What does the snow remind you of? When birds and animals cross it, they leave a script - can you speak that language? Or talk to yourself in it?

*

742. How many lorries per hour roll down to the garbage dump out there on the marshes, a rattling, bouncing stream of vans and pickups? This is where the marshes *used* to be, where seagulls peck at flapping rubber. And how many men work there with their gear, their headrags and plastic Pink Panthers for walking-stick handles? They eat their lunch in a tent right there on the compressed, flapping sea of rubbish, plates and flasks on an upturned crate. When you drive down there to make a drop, they pick their way through everything - what is the finest thing they've ever found?

799.   How many windows on your street gaze right into one another? Imagine yourself in the window directly opposite, looking at you.

800.   Are there secret rooms in your street, secret tunnels? Tell me where they are.

801.   How many buried rivers are there in your city? What do you see reflected in the water?

802.   Do window-panes reflect the sunset? Are they as red as the rivers?

817.   Have you heard the one about the crocodiles in the sewers? I have.

*

911.   In whose bedroom is most of the political power concentrated?

912.   Listen - is that the sound of cars or the sound of helicopters?

913.   Do either your dictators, or elected representatives, know that one day birch or palm will buckle and blow in the wind of what remains?

914.   Do they know their accounts will never add up however hard they try?

*

955.   Is there a decent poem written about your city?

957.   Can you find an ending then, to the city's poem?

958.   Is this question a *fair* question?

959.   Is it a *trick* question?

960.   Do willows sweep the waters of the lake like goose-wings?

961.   And do wasps swarm in a cloud around your beloved's window?

*

The Lives of The Saints

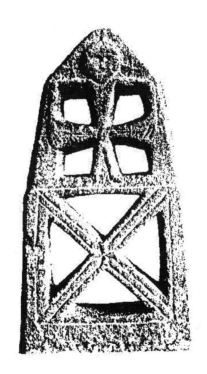

Cuthbert

Eadfrith's Work:

Clover and pebble-eggs
lace behind my quill –

the parchment is later stitched
and bound in goatskin,
bevelled and blood-warm-red
over beechwood stiffeners,

then this God's spell is boxed
in ocean pewter
and cobbled with glistening rocks.

This is God's signature,
Eadfrith's hand.

Enough for any life,
one such book.

+

The tides suspire,
bringing, and lifting away
the visitor.

This is an island's rhythm –

and that of the hermit,
convinced to become a bishop.

The tides come in and leave.

While there is time
the Word must be said out loud
as the sea on shingle.

Cuthbert – the jackdaw,
shipwrecked in body and soul –

Cuthbert – the sea threw a rooftree
onto a limbless strand,

an eagle tossed him a flapping fish.
God fed him.

+

The English, they are a rough and fierce lot
and worship rough and fierce gods.
This Saturday they drive a red and yellow rosary of cars
across the causeway, each individual heart engraved
with crossworks of laughter and secret rage,
of ageing, and complex sexual loves –
knotworks, which writhe toward symmetry.

+

My fingers are striving to follow the surge and weight of the
water-wave –
Godspeech,
line on,
rolling on,
line –

but Cuthbert stood up to his shoulders in it.
Those jackdaws provided a beak-full of pig-fat
for his boot-grease, left his thatch alone.
He moved immoveable stones
with God-muscle, flexing like fish.

+

Today I came across a little dish of gravel on the beach –
a kind of nest, with three neat eggs (of Oystercatcher?),
chalky, brown and blue-grey flecked.
They are replicas of pebbles.
We are as vulnerable and as camouflaged as that.

+

I spend my life
to exalt the Initials.
The rest of the words just follow.
This body is what we are capable of.

+

Relics

A lock of hair which glows like wire in the crucible

a fragment of Jesus's sponge

the claw, or the egg, of some monstrous bird.

A book.

Some fact, in a pulp of coffinwood and a jumble of yellow bones.

Some trust, in what you touch.

+

Tradition claims that a holy man named Issui had a cell nearby, probably in the dingle and near to the holy well still to be seen there. From his cell Issui instructed the people in the Christian Faith and won their affection. We can well imagine their distress when he was murdered by an ungrateful traveller who had received hospitality in his humble cell. Because of his reputation for sanctity and the esteem in which he was held, his cell soon became a place of pilgrimage, and the well which once nourished the saint was thought to possess healing properties. In the early 11th century a wealthy continental pilgrim was cured of his leprosy by the water in the well. In gratitude he left a hatful of gold to build a church on the hill above the well and this church was dedicated in the name of St. Issui.

from the 'The Church of Merthyr Issui at Patricio' by Canon Arthur Reed

Remains of Issui

My ochre is easily dug from the field,
my green from the finch's wing
when Spring is curative.

Lepers,
come.

Come everyone with rotten purse-strings

       here on the rood-loft
          vine-leaves sprout from the dragon's mouth,

       the dragon sucks
          the shoots of the vine –

and find a hatful of gold on the hilltop:
stems and shoots to boil for colour,
ink from Issui's lamp-soot.

Come
to this, the Blue Hole –

        below the sky, the hill,
        below the hill, his well;

the warm-honey smell
        of sawn grain,
a heron,
perched beyond his cell.

+

Says Issui
to every leper:

come,

consumptives, paymasters, singers with rotted strings,
to where the ash and the holly break
    from the dead bole of the yew

      – the leper's body:
          clumps of hard red wood in knee and brow,

      spurts holly,
        shining ash –

and ask for a fish from the heron's bill.
No traveller leaves unwashed, unfed;
one may kill, another bequeaths
a hatful of gold
      to build a church for Issui
        up the hill.

+

Vine-leaves sprout from the dragon's mouth,
the dragon devours
          the limbs and veins of the vine.

Says Issui:

my ochre is easily dug from the field,
my green from the woodpecker's wing,
my black from lamp-soot,
come

and see.

My toes may bump the crimson bones of the twisted yew,
my hair be snagged on fence-wire,
still my fingers burn this hole in the blue;

you lepers,
pursers,
hydrophobes,
verbicides,

come and feel.

+

Says Issui,
hear:

– comes
the singer
goes –

his glee is struck from a fret of black and gold.

+

In A.D.405, five years before the fall of Rome, St. Patrick carried the Gospels to Ireland. During two centuries of anarchy and confusion on the continent, the Celtic Church developed in a hard school of poverty and adventure, cut off from the mingled theology and politics of the Mediterranean world. In 563 St. Columba crossed to Scotland and settled on Iona and in 635 Aidan, one of the monks of his foundation, travelled eastwards, to found the island monastery of Lindisfarne.

The Celts have been reproached by Bede for their failure to evangelise the Saxon invaders. Had history allowed them to reply, they might have remarked on the Saxon reluctance to learn from a people they despised and had defeated, and it was perhaps to avoid this difficulty that Aidan trained twelve young Englishmen as missionaries, one of whom was Cedd.

In 653 Cedd landed on the quay of the old Roman fort of Orthona and travelled the kingdom of the East Saxons. After returning north for consecration as bishop, he came south again and built churches at Tilbury, Prittlewell and other places whose names are now lost. His principal foundation was a community at St. Peter's, Bradwell-on-Sea, which may be considered the first cathedral in Essex.

In 664, when the key differences between the Roman and Celtic churches were debated at the Synod of Whitby, Cedd, who acted as interpreter, adhered to Canterbury and to Rome. The authority of the Celtic church, with its integrity, its mysticism and its love of nature, retreated northward.

St. Cedd died of the plague at Lastingham in the Yorkshire Moors in October 664. When his people at Bradwell learned that he would visit them no more, thirty of them journeyed up the coast and all but one, a boy, shared his end.

adapted from 'The Fort of Orthona and the Chapel of St. Peter-on-the-Wall, Bradwell-on-Sea, Essex'
by H. Malcolm Carter

St. Cedd Talks In His Sleep

The plague / how amiable are thy tabernacles Lord of Hosts /
the current washes up signs for creatures of the sea like me
to eat and rubs away the shore, exploding the skin of my face
and the bone of the shore / I faint for the Courts of the Lord

my elbows are wrinkled and cracked, the skin around my eyes
as hungry as thieves + as thieves in Winter / bird-tracks scuttle
on the quicksand of my chest, these signs erupt in the cave of
my holy head

this is where I live /
my delirium
deliberation

+

The sea recedes and reaches
into the cracks and shallows of my face
rip-tide pelts my + pelts my bones with grit
they freeze in Winter

this will be known as erosion /
this will be known as the plague of silver-foil /

the merciless psalm

this / my disappearance
+ pearance

+

My soul cries out
my fish-oil candle

the focus tightens
and fixes a future
a car in a square / an advertisement
no / it becomes a limousine
parked in the square of an ancient court
I see that the country is as poor as I am
the people collect in droves to have their photos +
photos taken / see themselves
in a distorted + torted mirror
tanks will roll into that selfsame square at night

Is this the way it will be
or the way it has always been?

My fingers wrinkle and crack, the
skin around my eyes is map of Winter criminals /
the starling pecks at the breadboard of my head

I will die of the plague in 664 / I have walked
+ will walk to / built + have built
a cathedral / and a tiny chapel
out on the sea-wall / Bradwell
to bear the bulk of the Lord

this is my disfigurement
my display

+

The sun rubs into my flesh like fish-oil /
backbone wrenched with sand
erodes the cliffs, my face,

the thigh-bone of the land

What do the cormorants say?
– the sea is full of fish
/ and fish must feed on something
the sea is overflowing with the Living and the Dead

What do the stars?
/ say Heaven is wide
enough for all the souls that have ever lived on Earth
the starfish talk about sex
my body clings without a thought like fog

the sandfly tells me what I am
and what I always was / a
starving wind from Eden

this is my disappearance
this is my drug

+

God sends messages in bottles
when I read them / swallow
the Word is a thing in Itself
like lichen
cormorant
finger-nails
belly
rip-tide
eating into the coast of my brain
and shaping it, fixing a future

I am an age of mirrors to come
where banks with windows + window of shining gold
and satellites flapping between the planets like silver-foil
will fornicate / breeding needs of sand

this is my delirium
this my disappearance

+

The voice which I get from Heaven
spake unto me said
Go and Take the Little Book
and Eat it Up *I* and It shall
Make thy Belly Bitter, but It shall be
in thy Mouth as Sweet as Honey

your hands push messages into bottles
His heart is an aerodrome at night
and you *I* are coming into land

and then

His heart is a quiet dockland street,
it is summer, grass grows up through the cobbles *I*
the houses are silent and full of folk

I have walked into English jungles
braved their teeth and spears

this is my delirium
dispen + dispensation

+

Science and Art should make you afraid
the length + the length of life
is nothing, living well

is everything *I* frozen +
frozen bodies in the mind of God
and human germs in test-tubes
are unanswerable questionmarks *I*
live well *I* and find your questions answered

I swallow the pages and know
to certain kingdoms will be given this excess
to others nothing *I* they will chew
the ashes of themselves

this is my drug
my difference

+

Crystals + crystals
spreading in chambers
waiting for rebirth, missiles
gnaw under rocks, the human particle
swarms in retorts before taking shape

Is this the future
or just forever?

Is it something to be
or the way it has always been?

This is my description
where I live

this is my deliverance
my dissemblance

+

God your face is an airfield /
blinking + king illuminated
we are coming into land
your hands are paths of crossed white chalk
your brain is a noisy sea

I feel the heathen drawing on the wall of the cave
using my fingertips
dimpled stone under sand and soot /

this glyph of a tottering ox
her back stuck with arrows
she totters and rocks

I endure + endure
the dance + the dance
of the hunter
the joy of the death-dance

This is where I live /
this cave is my eyeball
this wall / a nest in a niche
my soul / this carving
cut on my brain
like a birthmark

+

IONA

Colmcille

the
Red Flower
Hoodie Crow
North Wind
False Man

Colmcille

the Cave of Easter
Isle of Tangles
Height of Storm

I

0

N

A

Dove
Stranger
Flower
Cock

a Glass Ladder to God

Speaking Columba

Speaking Columba:

asking Columba
for greenglass stones
                 that are eyes
and white sand
                 that is skin
in saltwater light

Speaking Columba:

stones that are stippled pink
and sand that was once *coccolithopores*
1/200th each of a millimetre
miles of them spotted by satellite
drifting, a ghost off the coast of Stornoway

Speaking Columba:

this Saturday morning's miracle
is
          the white sand
              scattered

the teaching
          scattered

before there was need to teach

before the need

                    +

Speaking Columba:

I
   is Iona

              Dun-I
                    its highest point

I   itself
   is only memory

speaking Columba

                         Dove
                         Stranger
                         Flower
                         Cock

knotwork /
        refrain

of I
    & Other

speaking Columba

    the miracle this Saturday night
    is Ardmeanach, Ulva, Gometra,
    rippling north in late light

  Dun-I
    is a lump of machair

    before there is need to speak
    before the need

+

Columba

comes ashore

and pulls the spiral into himself
  of greenglass stones
   and white sand
  and stones that are rippled pink in saltwater light

he drags the spiral of 3 battles:

    Cul Dreamne
    Coleraine
    and Clonard

                crane-cleric
                        Ornithomancer

Columba stands on the Hill With Its Back
                        To Ireland
                hearing Morigen, raven-goddess
                        screeching out from the slatey
                                shoulder of Ben More

he twirls his finger
        tracking the flight of the gull in bright initials,
                syllables,
                        scribing the Cathach, a psalter

melting the sand of the thousands dead —

                Cul Dreamne
                Coleraine
                Clonard

to a twist of greenglass stones that are eyes
        and birdshead finials, knotwork of stones
                that are stippled pink and veined like skin

                        +

Speaking Columba:

here in the abbey
        by votary light

names are woven
                into a fisherman's net

hair
feathers
lichen

Mrs. Lewis, Mr. Johnson

'bad blood',
'bereaved',
'Inoperable'

scraps of paper
heart conditions

loves and shreds of the woven world

+

Speaking Columba:

here
before there is need to teach
before there is need to speak

God is a zoomorph

shape-shifter

speaking Columba

+

Columba travels the length of the Great Glen to carry the faith to the heart of Pictland:

I

their arrowheads are delicate –
azure, rose, and ashen-lemon

fine –
they finger them like moth-wings

spell Iona –

pink thrift,
rust in a rock-pool

gannet
stuck to a standing-stone

syllable sticks to syllable –

but he who puts his faith in the causal
carves the cross

I guide you into the ranks of gestures

I-Chalium-Chille,

called now Columba

*

"Ere the world come to an end
Iona shall be as it was"

      − from The Prophecies of Columba

May 1992

Cloch Cennau / Cennau's Bell

".......directing her journey beyond the Severn and there meeting with certain woody places she made her request to the Prince of that country that she might be permitted to serve God in that solitude. His answer was that he was very willing to grant her request; but that the place did so swarm with serpents that neither men nor beasts could inhabit in it. Presently prostrating herself in fervent prayers to God, she obtained of him to change all the serpents and vipers there into stones. And to this day the stones in that Region doe resemble the windings of Serpents through all the fields and villages...

Many years being spent by her in that solitary place, the holy Mayd returned to the seat of her nativity. Where, on the topp of a hillock seated at the foot of a high mountain she made a little habitation for herself; and by her prayers obtained a spring there to flow out of the earth; which by the merits of the Holy Virgin afforded health to divers infirmities..."

At Cennau's Well

What's my name?

Is it Cennau
    Keyne
        Keyne-wiri?

Whatever it was, I lost it across the estuary,
      I dropped it in that desart place the other side of the
                                Severn,
     driving the serpents into the stones,
       deriving a kind of silent heaven

and now my name is just a place
      where jets and lorries clamber throughout my
        clouds, vibrate my bridges –

What's my name?
Is it Ceneu
    Keyna the Virgin
        Keyne?

and what's this place but a bigger body,
     a musculature of stones and beasts and jungled ridges?
       Whatever the name, I am now become this territory,
                           such as —

        foxhole,
           steppingstone,
          dyke,
            and ditch

I am become its bell, and my mouth will be buried,
   stuffed with leaf and twig, and rich with spider and silver worm

my Father-God will always burn –

I am his bell and was rung before the mechanic, the
     metalled road, I sung when even the church
was only a glade of stubble, a slab of stone with sockets
    for oil and water, a congregation of speechless rubble

I am a daughter of red-haired Brychan,
  daughter of burning –

      before the roadmap, almost before the furrow,
          I fixed this oratory (log for lintel, twisted branch
             for a roofridge –
      shoulder and backbone)

the first smoke of the valley rose from my circle of stones

and now a fox is winking at the window, an otter tumbles and
         churns throughout my blood –

    I married this wood.

+

I married this wood –

and beat my tongue in prayer like tempering bell-metal
— slow-worm soul-work – beating a blade
to hack a path
through plagues of brambles,
the body's jungles.

When I was south of the Severn, "that desart place",
I cured an epidemic, freezing the snakes into
ammonites –
but now I know that the codes of the corn and
the river will twist
and swell for ever, things will always fall in love
with soil and water, crawl into bed with fire –

tonight, the lips of the fire and water whisper
"Take and eat – this is my body"

but here there is no mirror
but rain-drenched rock, no love-lamp but the

whinchat's breast –

I am Keyna the Virgin, and whisper my vespers to crowded sky
and wet black soil –

I am Cennau – a river in anger,
Keyne-wiri the buzzard,
circling to rest

+

I am his loophole
  foxhole
    dyke
      and ditch

  his pier
    steppingstone
      ditch
        and shield

      his scrivener
      index
        grapnel
          lifebuoy
            gin

So how can my service today be anything other than these –
  each letter a scribbled sun-stitch?

Slowly as serpents, the words uncurl,
  the loin-pressure twists, unfurls
    and every phrase and cob in the drystone wall
      that stammers across the pasture
  knows that the code of the corn and the clouds, the law of
                                genetic cities,
    the clasp of the body's book,
      will be broken,

      the Word will awaken.

              +

Cennau's Medicine

China clay
            bevelled and pressed by the potter's thumb –

    the eyes are sprung!

        she leaps into the world

                        +

            it is con/fusion to him who comes to be
                        looked at –
                her eyes skewif, her ear
            tilts to an osprey's shriek
                                    in a distant gin

                        +

        her one eye rests upon you

            leaves

                like a crow's wing

            dusting snow

                        +

she knows a man's shadow's
a handle
for ghosts to grip

to lift him
out of the world –

she feels his rocking shoulder and the sliding,
agonising vein
sees each and every blink in the dazzling
Suit of Lights

+

she knows –
his need of the ball-court,
his joy and terror
to lift aloft the embroidered stave,
the gilded buckle,
the goggling head

+

and so, this girl is gagged by the witch of plague
this tribe misplaced their king –

its ancestors are stalking through the hallways
hanging by their heels
from rain-drenched thatch

+

the badger knows his patch of earth
　　the otter smears his tar-marks on the guidance-stone

but we know one another,
　　need a ritual strong as ringing bone

　　　　　　　　+

　　　her mind is with the grass-waves,
　　　　　jumping with the river-fish

or startled, like a game-cock
　　shattered from grasses,
　　　a driven pig

　　　she charges the dirt-path's loop
　　towards her oratory – here the roof
　　is thatched with hair
　　　　　and a twisted back for a ridge

　　　　　　　　+

　her takes you in at face-value,
　　　fish-bone lipped, her eye ignites
the leaves and branches of your skin –

　　　ablaze you know the kindness of the
　　　　　body-bell,

　　its tapering ring

　　　　　　　　+

.... But when the time of her consummation approached she saw in a vision as it were, a fiery pillar, the base whereof was fixed on her bed. Now her bed was the pavement strowed over with a few branches of trees. And in this vision twoe Angels appeared to her, one of which appeared to take off the sackcloth with which she was covered and put on her a smock of fine linen, and over that a tunick of purple, and last of all a mantell all woven with gold.

Therefore sending to her nephew Saint Cadocus, she said to him: 'This is the place above all others beloved by me; here my memory shall be perpetuated. This place I will often visit in spirit if it be permitted mee. And I am assured it shall be permitted mee because our Lord has granted mee this place as a certain inheritance.
My tombe shall lie a long time unknown...'

from Cressy, quoted in 'Notes on the Church and Parish of Llangenny, Breconshire'
by A. Raymond Hawkins

Cennau's Passing

Linen

sparrow-shroud

in January: lights from porches,
putting away of cars at night

starving for something dry and green

+

Purple

"My bell is dimpled, cisted at the shoulders,

(a hot Spring day, the pulse in spiking leaves)

it waits to shed its spider-studded skin
for fourteen hundred years –

my rhetoric gathers and swarms
and then you know me –

the sword and the soul of things,

this clearing"

+

Gold

Fever.

The stitch at at the edge of a leaf.

+

Llangenny   1993-94

Hephaestus

He talks to you in a Black Tongue
they are filled with smoke
his words
his mind is blue
he is beating the words
    to tame the words
he is beating beating
the   damn   words
his mind is black & blue
and his tongue is flame
blue flame

I am talking to you
and my mouth is smoke
and my language is blackened & yellow with smoke
my teeth blue-black
I am beating the words
and his mind it is hot as hammer
as cold as anvil
redyellow damndamn heart
and what is he beating
the sun
        is shriek
on the hammerface
torn to a cockerel-
            blade
to shreds of shine on shine

his tongue is black
and he talks
        his tongue
is in your black mouth
I swing my hammer
white-hot iron
bursts
between surface and surface
your mouth is a bath that

sizzles as he dips
his burning metal in

Damn your banging syllables are black & yellow-white
are blue and shrieking gas
I beat the heart
damn heart
the lungdrum
black is burnt as roof of straw
is melted onto benches, walls
my mouth is bubbled & scorched
    he sings

with lips of love

                    *

In the middle of Africa
born
again & again
in Greece, Cathay
and again
in a sodden Scottish glen
a cwm
a Pennine dale

a cripple
        again and again -
I was mashed by a stallion's heel in the belly
or maybe under-cooked

and this is my life

                    my dysfunctional family

this is my name

                - Hephaestus

was taken in care
grew finger-skilled
with moth's wing wire
    & watchsprings

        fucker
        father
           drop me
        out of the bedroom window

        dangle me
          my fate to fall

    *

working in the steelworks every day
      my callipers clatter up and down the works canteen

by night
    I weave a net of springs & cogs
to catch my Love

to free from arms of War
    her love

which is a nest of softest stars

    *

Coal-lust

    and fire-lust

steel-lust

I do my job as best I can
        with fire
    and clay
        and iron

I beat what human shapes I can
     the ugly jeweller
   drum-maker
     forger

                  – blades for soil and blades for limb,
                      a clutch of bells and javelins
            as black as any January dawn
                  when mallet rings on scalding chain
            and torque and arrowhead,
                 thrust into rust-skinned water,
                   sing!
                     to know their purpose

       *

without my Fire
there is no Axe
no Helmet
Spear
Adze
Spade
no Crop
no Mask
no House is shapely jointed

but for the blade that rings in the time and the truth of its use
no way is cleared
Meat brought down
no Furrow ploughed
no Furrow ploughed in the soul of the enemy

God the Thunderer

He Who Bends And Buckles Even Kings

Who Gives And Rots

Who Exists of Himself

The One Who Meets You Everywhere

Forger of Feet and of Hands in the Furnace

Jeweller of Nail and Lip

       *

Jewel and cripple,
I cripple and jewel the world

        I procreate with wedge & mallet
           skewer, stylus, tine –
       it's me to blame for all the cuts
           that time demands

            I dress your neck & eyes
              with sequins, microscopically honed,
            to show you how
              my Fire-World is reproduced in you.

     *

Without my rage
there is no Change –
the tool, the blade, the ornament we are
is cast,
re-cast
and shows no print of its former life

save always:

God the Thunderer

Giver of Breath

the Giver of Sun and of Rain

the Inexplicable Spider

the Giant Sea, Whose Headdress is the Horizon

He Who You Can Lean On And Not Fall Over

the Bow in the Sky

the One Beyond All Thanks

       *

from Tilt

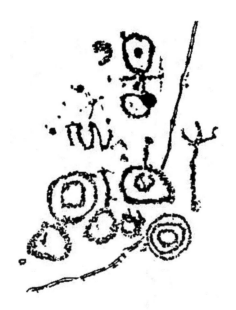

First Moon: at the Dragon's Head

..........*ssiang!*

daylight –

stroking the silver strings

*

listen –

mist –

sifting the stones and reflective laurel

the house a heron

rising out of the black pool

*

…..ssiang!

I wake again from a dream of ruins

this house is a book -

chimney

window

roof

scalp

& eye

& tooth

*

somedays we see the herons along the river —

where do they sleep I wonder?

and how the ancestors?

if they're not planted fast, it's said

their hair will grow for ever

somewhere the heron lifts like light

from the black river

*

                    path

                    and wall

                    and crocus shoot

                    vein

                    and rib

                    and foot

a shovel clangs on far-off tar
a sparrow singing

            "here
             I was born"

*

the Winter dawn

stroking her silver strings

*

Note to First Moon:

"The songs contain a number of meaningless cries or exclamations, and at the caesura of each line is the exclamation hsi which may represent the panting of the shaman in trance... One might expect the Spirit to speak through the shaman's mouth. The shaman, says a writer of the first century A.D., 'strikes the dark strings' (probably a shaman name for a kind of zithern) and brings down the dead who speak through his mouth."

Arthur Waley,
in his introduction to
*The Nine Songs: A Study of
Shamanism in Ancient China.*

Sky Burial: Skirrid Fawr

At the end of the Shining Path, along the ridgeback,
there is a sharper rise to the peak. The falling fields
were misty, the ridge was yellow and a pair of crows
were perched ahead of us as black and big as vultures.

They took off. The last time we came here there was
thin ring of ashes around the pinnacle; we ate a picnic,
and I was absent-mindedly fingering them before I real-
ised what they were. By then they had mostly filtered
into the turf. The shuddering blue of a tilted beetle
clambering over the grasses; a thick, red, lazy erecting
bull.

It feels like a place for an Autumn sky burial, meaning a
wide sculpture of time and material: a curling cloak of
blondish grass; a bull's breast stuffed full with feathers; a
crown of ashes.

*

Woodpecker, if you are anywhere near, nail me a
house, and everybody bring up stones, as if to a cairn,
to hold a shape against the brain's dissolving.

The fields spread out to the bluff and the eyes revolve;
patterns of rock and cloud and hand that fall again to a
different colour.

Questionmarks At Bredwardine Churchyard

"The day lifted itself like a muddy cow from the sunny
                                        field,
its head in a cloud of flies" is written.
As soon as I opened my eyes, I saw the world outside
                                    the caravan
in all its likelihood - that oak is as dense as the year has been
and will be, further afield – the stumpy vertical
at Arthur's Stone is like a standing man,
the capstone like a fallen, charted man
with hard white lichen, good a map as any
of the geography, the life and death
of any weighty man, or country,
                                        split in its fall.

The stone itself is continent of signatures:

        AAL
        Aug 5
        HRL
        1901

– it must have taken a long, long hour
to cut their glyphs this tight
– "AAL" a certainty, an increment to stone.

The metaphors go on – as rash as this pink moss
which spreads with every May –
        "this map is the face of a deadman,
this fly is the sound of a hand,
that beechtree swells like a scalp,
that crop, it looks like a language,
folded and cut –"
                        and the palm-smoothed effigy
of Walter Baskerville in stone defaced,
his face replaced with a stone.

*

Shape-changing: what is the truth of the
lintel at Bredwardine? – the "Bird-man"
(is it a Dog-man?) wearing a cassock (is that it?),
next to a "Monkey" (in childbirth posture?),

something like Sheelagh-na-gig, his
crooked arms aloft like
holding an invisible trapeze
or binary poles, by which device
to stake, or map, his territory –

Some certainty: "This is a Doorway"
(now it is filled with stone) –
                                "Consider as You Enter,
What You Enter, Constitute..."

*

Question - is there a figure, worn beyond knowing,
next to the Bird-Man-Dog-Man in that space of yellow stone?
I mean to say, is that where a figure would fit?
A penny-size patch of pale green lichen blossoms right of the
                                monkey's breast,
cloud-shadow strokes the hillside.
Here in the poem, this is appropriate.

*

And what were gargoyles, misericordes really for?
Not just to hold up the snoring arse of a priest
or decorate a rain-mouth, pissing rain
but on the crown of a pillar or, as here, above a doorway, saying
"Enter, If You Think You Mean It, And Consider Where You Are,
The Language That You Are, The Metaphors
That You Are Free To Use"

*

Children, ducks and cattle in the farmyard
spread across the mind, as good a map as any,
opening.
        We walk the hillside path
and watched by an early owl and the eye of the bluff
we come again, to eat and drink
and talk of monsters, love, and making a living.

*

The Geomancer

I know the lie of the land,
its bone and blood
the back of my hand,
the run
       of the black and the white water.

Here's my gourd,
my blanket,
and my man of straw
to shield you from the living face
of the demon dead –
I stand my ground at the Dragon's Head.

Listen –
  I exhale the buried cities –
Cambalu and Samarkand by Oxus,
Paquin, Negus and Melind,
Battersea, in rainy winter evening's green and yellow lights
  – I strike the strings.

My song is just a territory
being shaped, becoming known.
My chant accelerates like water
falling, black and white,
  through streambed stones.

I know the lie of the land,
my head and hands
  your mountain and your wood.
Their steps,
  their doorways opening and shutting
in your heart
  let drift your bone and blood.

St. Martin's Church, Cwmyoy

for the New Year, 1994

The earth is rucked by thousands of years of landslip –
   the "Cwm of the Yoke" – and ridden with mud after weeks of rain.

  St. Martin's Church is riven, but bucks at every side
the quick and the slow storms
   of weather, expression, geology –

this is the kick of recurring discovery:
   twisting words or wrenching clay
     to mould some truth from the groundswell –

one by one, we climb the quivering ladder to shadows and bells.

An Exile's Letter

These are my rooves and bridges
     these my tracks in mud –
   this is my radio
      mopping the people's rage,
I turn the river's page

        (which is, after all, as good as mine –
        for every day I drag my fuel from its edges)

           the mountain's ditches

           and silver stones

           are daily,

           syllable by syllable,

           becoming known –

        I learn their forms,
           their forms of patience,

                working alone.

The Invaders

Defeat: A Javelin

(from a Northern river, the memory-frontier of a Roman soldier slain in battle)

But listen, I have forgotten –
     my life is a skyful of moonlight covered with cloud,
  a yellow ghost
        patrols the midnight limit

I speak, but I have forgotten –
     my brain is a hillful of trees, their roots ripped up
        by a wind that slammed into my helmet
            with your javelin –

                  *

   So, I lost my head –
     it floated down the channel
keenly observed by a Kingfisher.

No, it's better not to wear this necklace of shimmering roads,
        this head-dress of hills
     and the signs that swerve in the midnight sky

when they all insist on a time like this –
        our teeth like fallen bridges,
our voices the tremble of owls.

The shields and the poles of our enemies clogged and stirred
the stream –

our army died on television,
buzzing, in a pool of dots,
the papers full of photographs of peasants
stripping down the implements and emblems of our law

No, it's better not to know the language any more –
we came to bring a mountain's law to the hills
and highways to the pitted tracks.

Now the moon is rattling in its socket,
our speeches bleach and dissolve
against the bluff.

*

We got this far.

The rivers of the North roll on
to the unattainable coast.

*

Victory: A Dance On The Llywel Stone

our prow pushes open
    the summer river –
       starlings and lanterns

*

push between fields which ripple and comb –
    Maccutrenus! –
        we've snapped off the head of your
          one black rock
    and stuck it the other way up

*

our insect eyes patrol the purple
            hedges
  (summer holly),
     speaking in ripples and kites
        a zigzag of sweatmen and stickmen
        and cattle,
           ours! –
  cracked between cwms and garns

*

our speeches rage and dissolve
    over Mynydd Troed
where I was manned,
    shaking my javelin's pearls from its tip

*

worldwork –
   one by one
the stonesweight
   in the pasture wall

   your curses fuel it

*

At Kilpeck Church

These Herefordshire carvers hacked into stone
                as if it were daylight,

freeing such as a "bear", that devours "children"
a "bird", that regurgitates something
into a "human" mouth,

an angel, falling from spacetime,
knot of stone.

These men of Herefordshire knew what they were doing,
                chewing stone as if it were night and day.
The rain behaves like love or leprosy,
pouring from lips yanked wide
in grins or is it grimaces?
splashing centuries of
craving,
laughing,
swearing, by day and night.

This Friday afternoon, the two of us standing here,
straining for detail,
knotting the branches of torment and insight.

(for Richard Lanham)

The New Year

The year began like a damp fox
stretching its paw from the hedge.
We slept till late, and when we rose
the valley to the south was full of mist,
the sky above the mountains yellow in the rain.
Sparrows scratched the tin on the caravan roof,
the trees stood cold and empty,
rising from their hoops.

Walking the River Wye our minds,
beside each other, drifted – when we spoke it tended to be of
the same thing at the same time.
This was the 80's, when wealth
was gathered to the businessmen, the gamblers –
                        Tao Yuan Ming
lay scorn on every aspect of government business,
tending his path and pasture, rewarding his friends for their help
with a bottle of wine.

The river was full to its banks and grey
with the strength of an army.
South, in Gloucestershire, the trains were blocked
and could not pass.
                        He wrote:
"The empty boat glides on –
whoever comes must go –
the ups and downs can never touch our freedom,"
emptying his jug of Kiangsi wine.

And drinking wine all night
they poured themselves over the ancient poems
sorting out all the differences of interpretation.

The river was glancing
through gullies and hedges,

regarding us, retreating
under an iron sky, that twisted,
turning like an ancient poem.

*

(for Ursula Frank)

Knotwork

1. The Font At Eardisley

The Rescue:

Slanting towards the left, away from the lion,
(good or bad, with his good and his bad
eye)
is it Jesus
pulling the man away?
        He is sloping, flying,
Jesus clutching his wrist
and around his feet are the lacing knots

which is *the Book*

that pulls to further, never-ending knotting,
timeless binding of cause-and-effect.

It is branches,
        branches and serpents,
armour,
        and leaves that are also armour.

Is it a saint
that clutches this book to his breast?

The Soldier

and the knots go on.
The soldier hides
in branches, yet he is bound in them,
convulsed in them, since Eden.

Every day
his spear ruptures the enemy's thigh,
they are plaited in fighting

and this wound,
                    or this killing,
could be where the carver started, or

the Lion

following them.
                  The wound leads on to the lion,
the font is a chasing, a bowl
of roads and sinews
looping through Saxony,
Angle-land's eastern fields,
the North and West.

I am, the carver says, a Viking and a Celt,
a writhing catholic from Spain
through Parthenay-le-Vieux perhaps
to here, Herefordshire.

Nobody knows my name.

I am the carved,
     my sinew-strings, my heart-knots
will finish as Shobden's soft pink arches –
weathered, no longer readable things.

2. Kilpeck

There is no way out of the eating,
Kilpeck's virgin/whore is all devouring,
all disgorging

– "this is my body."

She says let loose your monkey-mind
and let it dance
from knot to knot:

where fish eats man
eats bear
is fish

eats bird
is foliate head
is falling man

who plunges to ecstasy,
plunges to ego,
to eating,

to Image

– "this is my sex, my visage."

Only my ritual work, the carving says,
resolves the process:
Kilpeck's beakheads, smiling, birthing

– take and eat.   This is it, my body.

Get up close and trace the knot with your fingertip,
          your dog-eared notebook, close-up lens,
and stroke the joys and the sufferings

– this is my double sex, of eye and chisel,
something of the god you bring.

3. Temple Guardians, Kunming, South China

We howl slaughter
we tread lions
stretching our mouths to ferocious deltas.

Earlobes wrenched to shoulders,
eyes globes being sucked from orbit,
ribs waves, thrashing on mountains,
waves of mountains.

Darts and charges twist in our fingers
banners fume about our necks.
          On the stiff wind
              of our will and volition
we brandish hoops of forgotten purpose,
serpents, dragons, fiends, and tiny spheres for unknown reasons

no-one can pass us by –
there is no getting past the mirrors that catch the sun in
our chest and foreheads,

no getting past your face.

And when it's done the poem
leans or lies like a carved ball —
curlicues and drifts of stone
and oak-leaves wreathing a smiling face,
propped on a pillar, or flat on the winter floor
                              of Abbey Dore

Love & other poems

Cathedral Bells and 3 Mexican Postcards

Mixtec skull –
a blue mosaic of semi-precious stones
intact: a row of teeth.
The eyes like hubcaps.

Pyramide del Sol, San Juan –
another perfect form, the dust
erected into blood

                        – the steps –

                        – the Sun! –

And yet we hardly felt a thing,
the place was swarming with *'touristas'*
panting to the top,
and children from the shacks
which line the factory walls of Mexico City
hassling us with *"relics... ...gen-u-wln... ...senor... ...senora...*
                                        very cheap.. ...au-ten-tica..."

The 3rd –
a woman
taking the Big Knife
to her foot, picks out
a splinter, the landscape –

Cadence of bronze from the Gothic mass,

a rising vapour
(recognised as fear of the police)

Dead Cat In A Grocery Bag

("All men, take care, take care, Great Desert!")*

The teeth show –
that's the clearest sign of death.

The manner of its trashing –
     thrown from a car
     like putrid freezer-waste
               shows signs
of other death:

          a nest of blackened bones
that Kali (she who is the sleep of all) would love
to wear as amulets, or strung along her apron

but that she would *dance*,
and cannot
          weighted down with meagre rot as this.

* *an ancient warning etched in a rock face*
overlooking the Mojave desert

Desert Poem

ditches and dried-up beds

in the pale rock of the Earth,

blistered air

around the car

– pre-formal modality of cosmic matter –

"Shit, man,
don't stop the car on the highway!"

"5 bucks a time man!"

a badger? here?
and maggots

gristle and tendon
come under his knife

"It's claws, man!
Claws!"

Craiglyn Dyfi: High Water Lake

First attempt we underestimated distance,
second , beaten back by weather
blowing through the horns
atop the falls, the wind
the wind was here before the river
grey, & full of shot

she pushes back the voice
into our mouths
she tears our masks
she serpent-spits us back
into the rock
between the horns
she spills and falls

the upper land is hers,
the season, hers the language, Labrys
swinging down the slopes in rain
conceals reveals the image
of the mountain Aron Fawddwy,
cuts us out of this
her territory

number 3 was clean
with snow around
& clear air, we got up early,
made the lake, the egg, by 3.
Was black. The mountains rose
all round & one of us
revealed himself as crow

the wreckage of an aeroplane

Locations

Sexy Cadbury –

'talking of trees
is almost a crime'?
they speak for themselves

they speak for themselves
in a sexual circle of wind –
the fort green-lit, &
long grass, lime, & thorn

she sleeps

leeward,
   buttercups, daisies,
huddled upon the embroidery

O navigate: the mind is
frail & fragrant

                              (Cadbury Castle)

                    *

feathers, feeling
free   & balanced

sycamores stalk on
stranded roots on Loch Tay shore
Eagle maybe, I don't mean
feathery clouds, the
mountains solid, rolling,
dim, I mean
the entire grain, I just said
feathers, & grain

kingly & green
of what
is speaking hand & cloud

& flame
& ice to come

(Perthshire)

*

bones,
   flintstones
blacken & crack
   in the fire

broken,
   fit the hand,
the edges
   & the slopes
of this entire
     landscape

     love
       is geographical

     beech-tree
      thanks

     we're here

(Cissbury Ring)

From King's Cross

To whom shall I speak today?
The Lord of Heaps devours the jungle
yellow dung stuffing the radio
smoking the same old stuff for months

To whom shall I speak today?
Waves of demons on brilliant fish
grasp the moon with telescopic hands
King's X incommunicado!

To whom shall I speak today?

> *half man and half drum*
> *play till the end of my song*

I'll talk to the Panther Man –
he told me to eat and run
the Bird Man told me not to get burned
To whom shall I speak?

The Lion Man told me to sniff out the game
the Ape Man to ride on the top of the train
the Chancellor moans for his blown cover

> *white buds distress his tongue*
> *river run till I end my song*

To whom shall I speak today?
The Lord of Heaps devours the forest

> *half man and half drum*
> *city in shadow and city in sun*
> *half man and half drum*
> *one hand up and one hand down*
> *and a stone in each*

Song

In China there's no time at all like the present
in Russia there's no time at all,
thousands of miles of harvest lights
thrown by the handful on carriage walls

America's wages of sin is death
there's one white cloud in the sky,
a cleaver stands upright disguised by wheat
waiting for glory to stroll on by

in England we possess the information
in Russia all the aerials are high,
in either place the editors get scrambled
and the papers printed off in iodine

in USA the river roll the river sings
the river roll, roll, roll, roll, roll,
somebody's gone and got lost in the desert
somebody's gone and got burned

our money is so elegant and simple
Chinese money colourful and slow,
forbidden cities nowadays permitted
but everywhere there's someplace no maps show

(for Mark Williams)

New Year (1989)

The Sun-Wheel is the Circulation of the Forces in the Body
Speech is also Changing Things
and irises come up each spring
and what they are is Useless, thereby Real

                    And Love's
the dragon's legs unclosing. Somebody says
the best sunglasses are when you can see the eyes
and the finest songs are those you forget the quickest

                         and Love
is painting eyeballs on Eternity.
This is the snake-year – hum and sweat
in muggy creases of the fields
turning the earth with our own bodies
leaves unfurling in the sun

        This is the muscle-year –
the wind sings on the edge of your arm
and hearts are dealt seen soft in the Dealer's shades

Lochs Hourn and Morar

Silence radiates out from isolated lochside houses
 — eagle power.
Sun on the mountains,
Sun on the water.

We do not live here, or play music for Li Po.
A yellow toad on the grass,
a blue dragonfly, gone.

Whatever the signs say
 — nobody owns the land
or the paths across it.

Silent circles spread from the isolate dwellings,
traffic of birds on water.

Day Hospital

The minute hand swinging
without a sound
– unfinished poem

*

"under-valued":

sparrow
singing in a gutter
full of moss

*

a place of my own –
no walls
no roof

*

weary,
the oak tree
aching to drop its leaves

*

drunks beget drunks
like ditches beget the rain

*

eclipsed black moon
is twice as strong

*

"talking of patterns,
that 1950's orange zigzag carpet —
that was the prime of my life!"

*

"Quick
is an ugly word
 — soon's more flow to it"

*

Coming home —
no walls,
no roof.
Where's supper?

*

Absence:

        "Daddy?"

*

     (Grove Rd. Day Hospital, Bristol)

Silver John

"When evening shadows lengthen, it is not difficult to believe that the reedy little tarn of Llyn Hilyn, near New Radnor, is haunted by the spirit of a murdered man whose body was thrown into it.

The murdered man was known as Silver John because of the silver buttons he wore upon his coat. By some he is said to have been a cattle drover, by others a skilful bone-setter and charmer, especially expert in curing sick animals..."

A Dream Song Of Silver John

I'll crack your joints stretched backward on a hay-bale,
then kick you good up the arse.
What's up?
                  I'll yank your neck like a goose.
What ails you,
                      that a kick in the balls wouldn't cure?
Crack your arm across your back
and haul you up like a bag of grass.
I'll double you up like a mouldy carpet from out of some old woman's
                                            kitchen.
I'll pull your spine so fast and straight you'll shoot all over the straw.
You'll yelp like a cock taking fright at a fox
it'll curdle the milk in the goat
and back'll pull out straight and your knuckles go off like a gun.
I'll kick your bladder around all over the barn.
and pummel your guts like a red-faced wife at the doughboard.
I'll claw them out and wrap them round your neck and pull

them tight
till –
I'll tear your wick off and feed it to frisky hens.
I'll tug off your toenails and use them for fishhooks.
I'll rip out your glottis and stick it in mine and sing your songs
then I'll go to your mucky house and and I'll murmur your own sweet
things
to your daughter and wife and son.
Your tongue'll make a supper cheap for your fat blue cat.
I'll suck out your eyes then stick them back the wrong way round,

      so when I'm done you won't know whether you're coming or
gone –

*

Walking

Silver John is wandering the lanes from Kington to Builth. He's covered himself with moons, which jingle between the hedges. Money moons, his pay for broken ankles, black blood, bedroom trouble. Owen pulled his shoulder out, heaving a calf from a big Welsh Black; Robson was born with a tangled leg, a spastic branch, half-ripped from his hip. Now they're slaving away in their barns again. And John has been and gone.

He pummels the living daylights out of you, stretched dreadfully over a bale. Now Silver John is treading his old familiar line, humming his circuit. He takes his time today, it's sunny, his collie scratches and twists on a yard of string.

His hair is matted brown, his jacket stitched from bits of a hundred others. He smokes his scut and mutters his songs, the fluttering of throatwings fills the familiar bending hill. He treads his tunes on scabrous heel and toe.

He understands cows and dogs, and one or two women say women. At sunset, his jingling racket sets fire to polished leaves along his way. Tomorrow a pint and a flake of silver to toss you over a lump of hay and ring your ears. But now we are walking along with John to the dark, later to be so secret and bold and loud in the whispers and oily light of a high valley cowshed.

*

His Sickness

Catch your own reflection in his buttons,
his 30x30 pieces.
Silver John's no saint,
    no healer,
    poet,
    priest.
Is not a man.

Silver John's mother put cakes all over your body,
    then chewed them, one by one,
her sin-eating song in her nose full seemly.

He doesn't inhabit a house,
   or flat,
   or tent,
   or van.
He doesn't live nowhere.

John absorbs your illness.
You name it:
   gut-rot, mad cow, second childhood.
Viruses beg him to let them come to him.

He prays for them to infect his songs
   so that no-one can understand him.
He makes up stories about his granny's drum,
his Japanese sister,
   the moon he embraced.
His tongue is as hot as a horseradish.

No Jobseeker's Allowance,
   SS snoops,
   nor Neighbourhood Watch for John.
No Boots the Chemist or Marks & Sparks or Currys
              frozen doorways.
Just an ague, and a walk, a walk, a walk.

Don't fret,
he won't tell anyone about
   your itch,
   your dizziness,
   your vacancy.
You're safe with him.

This money he wears,
   is a thousand mirrors
and after all,
   your offerings.

Lay hairclips then,
    and broken bits of mirror,
    corners of postcards,
    little plastic bulls,
    and smeared algae jamjars
down at his well, his watering hole.

Listen hard to the woodpecker,
learn his rattle.
And then to the tick of the wood beetle.

Welcome the moth to your thumb,
and the bat to your bedroom.

Stick your head in the fox's den
put Golden Syrup out for badgers.

Paint your breast with wasps.

Look after nature's people.

*

(I'm hating and holding tight another wound-schism, driving along in a swirl of domestic anger, till finally a phone call finally puts the world to rights and frees me to wander on, to further dwell on those shiny coins "that were his eyes", a coat completely drenched wherein his killers saw themselves reflected, protective mirrors.

    "The Radnor Boys pulled out his eyes..."

So why did they ring the bells? Getting shot of the scapegoat, the Judas, showing off his (no, that's our) blood-money, fear and jubilation, guilt and liberation, all drowned out in a golden, banging flood.

Scab-ridden kerb-crawler, free-loading cunt of the ditches, (might as well call them gutters). Who the hell did he think he is?

Well, he's a story.

Janice, an Irish woman, rings me up to talk about her stories: "In the last few days you see I've lost my sight, it happens from time to time since I had my stroke. Well, and I can't walk or write, so my carer Mary has to do it all. I tell it all to her and she writes it down for me and types it up."

In New Radnor church it occurs to me that the darkness that smote the world when Christ died was the horror of our not being looked upon.

"I'm sorry for ringing you up so early in the morning, but I lose track of time you see."

I wonder did John fear death by water?)

*

A Second Dream Song

Oak-roots heave at the gale-clouds
the sky is green and waving, full of fruit

Every babe is born with Deuteronomy on his buds
the sea is solid salt, as bare as brass

Every day a man goes fishing in his attic
helicopters flap about like gold-red fish in pools

Sailors, when they're hungry, far from home, eat fog
The King, that spider in a crown, craps oats

The sea pulls back, reveals the altar of the world –
inverted oak, its root-claws yanking at gales

*

(Ending up at the 'reedy tarn' Llyn Hillin, where John was drowned, to observe the molten, softly swaying, lemony green of the reeds and the splash and the dip and the cruise of the coots. Despite the cutting through of regular day-out traffic to Builth and the barbed wire fence, it's beautiful, shining blue in warm summer light, leaning against the benevolent slopes of today's story.

The blue, the green, the fawn and the steel of the fence and the red of the Citroen parked on the gravel, resolve themselves to the white of the only outcome that doesn't deny a thing.)

"...Some doggerel lines dating from about the time of the murder commemorate the crime, and in days gone by, it was asking for trouble to recite them within the hearing of a New Radnor man. The verse ran:

Silver John is dead and gone
So they came home a-singing;
The Radnor boys pulled out his eyes,
And set the bells a'ringing."

(Eric L. King)

*

Walking Towards His Death

Tonight my body's a tower of silence.
I'll die next Tuesday at half-past ten
not from cyanide or powdered granite
but tossed in a pond like a shit-tailed kitten,
an insignificant village.

Out beyond the coast there was a country,
ancient roads lead nowhere to it.
A thousand died at Cantre'r Gwaelod
the night Seithenyn, the floodgate guard,
got smashed on apple wine.
    Now axe-welts shimmer in lapping water,
clumps of hawthorn, willow, fir.
And teacups drip from fishermen's hooks.

Out beyond the coast of what we know
there's still a body, places that recur.
Tuesday, I'll gulp down
pulverised diamonds
and slap at the edge of your mind for good,
a silver fish.

*

Acknowledgements

Thanks to the editors of the following magazines and anthologies where versions of many of these poems have appeared:

Affirming Flame
Angels of Fire
Cabaret 246
Edinburgh Review
Fire
First Offense
Frames
Horizontal Volcano
Kite
Of Sawn Grain
Open World
Over Milk Wood
Poetry Wales
Reality Studios
Rhysling Anthology 1995
Strange Mathematics
Talus
The Pterodactyl's Wing
Wisdom Of The Crocodiles

Bronzes was published as a chapbook by the milvus-milvus press/ Charles St. Arts Foundation in 1987.

Six of these poems appeared in the book Turas, published by Red Sharks Press in 1988.

Ruan Ji's Island I (Tu Fu) In The Cities was published by Wellsweep in 1993 and draws on the poetry of the Chinese daoist Ruan Ji (210-263 AD), translated in collaboration with Wu Fu-Sheng. This collection was also published by Wellsweep in 1988, under the title Songs Of My Heart.

Tilt (also including work by John Jones and Ric Hool) was published by The Collective Press in 1996.

The Lives Of The Saints was published in a small edition by RWC (Read, Write, Create) to accompany a reading at *Subvoicive*, London in 1997

In Paradise

In Paradise, our faces become water,
there's plenty to drink —

In Paradise, we are all there,
animals, wandering down to the pool

*"arts and tongues are the cups
in which God drinks to us"*

– Sidrach Sympson 1693

How You Can Help

You can support The Collective by ordering any of our publications from your local bookshop, through your local library or direct from the address on the facing page. The money raised goes back into publishing and supporting poetry.

You can further support poetry through subscription to poetry magazines and by attending poetry readings at venues throughout the UK. Look out for Collective run events or, if you would like one in your area, get in touch with the Events Organiser, address as before.

The Collective

welshwriters.com

The Collective is a non - profit - making organisation formed in 1990 to promote and publish contemporary poetry. Funds are raised through a series of poetry events held in and around South Wales. The backing and generosity of fellow writers is a cornerstone of The Collective's success. Vital funding comes from public bodies including the Arts Council of Wales and donations are often received in support of the movement from members of the public. If you would like to contact The Collective to offer help or support then please write to:

The Co-ordinator

The Chief Editor

Events Organiser

or the

Distributions Officer

C/O

The Collective
Penlanlas Farm
Llantilio Pertholey
Y-Fenni
Gwent
NP7 7HN
Wales
UK

fish